Everyone Plays
Games

Aimee Popalis

rourkeeducationalmedia.com

Scan for Related Titles
and Teacher Resources

Teaching Focus:

Endings- *ed* –*ing*- Locate the words played and jumping in the book. Write the words and underline the root word. Then compare the endings. Can you add the –*ed or* –*ing* to each word? How does each ending change the meaning of the root word? Practice using the endings with another root word.

Before Reading:

Building Academic Vocabulary and Background Knowledge

Before reading a book, it is important to set the stage for your child or student by using pre-reading strategies. This will help them develop their vocabulary, increase their reading comprehension, and make connections across the curriculum.

1. *Read the title and look at the cover. Let's make predictions about what this book will be about.*
2. *Take a picture walk by talking about the pictures/photographs in the book. Implant the vocabulary as you take the picture walk. Be sure to talk about the text features such as headings, the Table of Contents, glossary, bolded words, captions, charts/diagrams, or index.*
3. *Have students read the first page of text with you then have students read the remaining text.*
4. *Strategy Talk – use to assist students while reading.*
   - *Get your mouth ready*
   - *Look at the picture*
   - *Think…does it make sense*
   - *Think…does it look right*
   - *Think…does it sound right*
   - *Chunk it – by looking for a part you know*
5. *Read it again.*
6. *After reading the book, complete the activities below.*

Content Area Vocabulary
Use glossary words in a sentence.

board games
festivals
generations
portable
technology
video games

After Reading:

Comprehension and Extension Activity

After reading the book, work on the following questions with your child or students in order to check their level of reading comprehension and content mastery.

1. *What are some outside games people play? (Asking questions)*
2. *Who can you play games with? (Summarize)*
3. *What kinds of games do you play with your family? (Text to self connection)*
4. *Why are traditional games important to the players? (Infer)*

Extension Activity

Think about your favorite games. What do you like about each one? Try to take your favorite parts of each of those games and create a brand new game! What are the rules? Do you play it outside or inside? Do you have a special board to play it on? What pieces or equipment do you need? How do you win? Gather your family and friends and have them play your game.

What games do you like to play?

Games are fun to play with your friends, family, or on your own.

Chess and other **board games** are played by moving special pieces on a board.

People in Russia have played chess for more than 1,000 years.

Some games can be made with things you find at home or outside, such as chalk, scarves, or sticks.

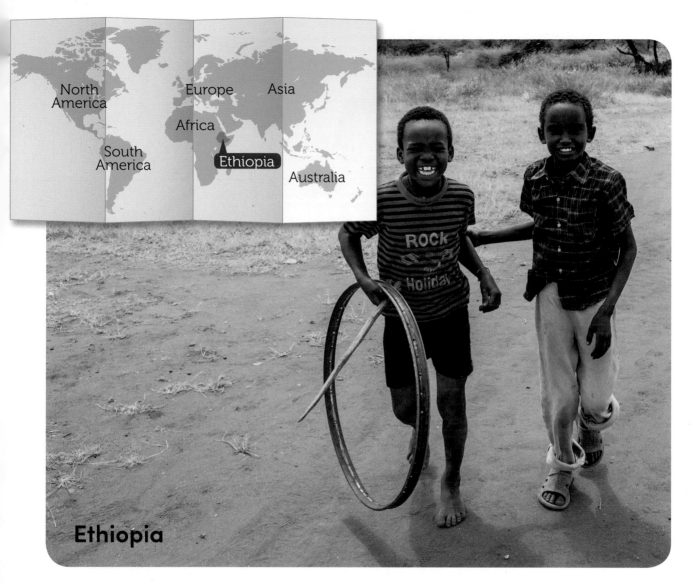

Ethiopia

In Ethiopia, children play hoop rolling games with the objects they find.

India

Video games use **technology** and electricity. People everywhere can play video games on televisions, computers, and smartphones.

Japan

Using the Internet, you can play games with kids in Japan, India, and other places all over the world!

For some games, all you need is your imagination.

Malaysia

Congkak is played in Malaysia. Dreidel is popular in Israel. Traditional games like these have been played for **generations**.

Israel

Mexico

People play games at home, school, parties, and **festivals**. Breaking a pinata is a traditional game at Mexican celebrations.

Portable games can travel with you no matter where in the world you are.

Thailand

Some games are played on a playground. Children in Thailand like to play jump rope games.

China

Quiet thinking games like mahjong are often played indoors. Mahjong was first played in China in the early 1900s.

Card games are great rainy day fun.

Whatever game you choose, the goal is to have fun. Let's play!

Photo Glossary

 **board games** (bord GAMZ): Games played on a board, such as checkers or chess.

 **festivals** (FES-tuh-vuhls): Celebrations that mark special days or events.

 **generations** (JEN-uh-RAY-shuhnz): People born around the same time period.

portable (POT-tuh-buhl): Able to be carried or easily moved.

technology (tek-NAH-luh-jee): A man-made tool, machine, or piece of equipment that does a job.

video games (VID-ee-oh games): Electronic game in which a player controls pictures on a computer or television screen.

Index

Show What You Know

1. What are traditional games?
2. What are some games that people play around the world?
3. Do you prefer quiet games or active games? Explain your answer.

Websites to Visit

www.web.archive.org/web/20130523212246/http://playgroundfun.org.uk
www.thehenryford.org/exhibits/toys
www.parents.com/fun/games/educational/games-from-around-the-world

About the Author

Aimee Popalis is a preschool teacher in Florida. When she was a little girl she loved playing games with her grandmother and inventing new games, like roller-skate basketball, to play with her brother and her neighborhood friends. Now, she still enjoys playing games with her family and she adores creating new games to play with her students.

Meet The Author!
www.meetREMauthors.com

© 2016 Rourke Educational Media

www.rourkeeducationalmedia.com

PHOTO CREDITS: Cover: © Bojan Kontrec, Matt Ramos; Title Page: © ideabug; Page 3: © Lifesizeimages; Page 4: © Africa Images; Page 5: © Mypurgatoryyears; Page 6: © Diane Labombarbe; Page 7: © Shape Charge; Page 8: © assalve; Page 9: © Martchan; Page 10: © ranplatt; Page 11: @ Siwasan; Page 12: © Andrew Rich; Page 13: © Yuri Arcurs; Page 14: © Masuti; Page 15: © Golden Pixels LLC; Page 16: © Todd Warnock; Page 17: © Monkey Business Images; Page 18: © tomgigabite; Page 19: © Tomas Skopal; Page 20: © Matjaz Boncina; Page 21: © Wojciech_gajda

Edited by: Keli Sipperley
Cover and Interior design by: Tara Raymo

Library of Congress PCN Data

Everyone Plays Games / Aimee Popalis
(Little World Everyone Everywhere)
ISBN (hard cover)(alk. paper) 978-1-63430-360-6
ISBN (soft cover) 978-1-63430-460-3
ISBN (e-Book) 978-1-63430-557-0
Library of Congress Control Number: 2015931687

Printed in the United States of America, North Mankato, Minnesota

Also Available as:

ROURKE'S
e-Books